The Ultimate Career Pocket Guide

THE ULTIMATE CAREER POCKET GUIDE

Francine Parham & Dolores DeGiacomo

Editor: Super Copy Editors, New York, NY
Photo credit: Deirdre Ryan Photography; photographer Deirdre Ryan

Notice of liability: The authors of work do not guarantee outcomes and are not liable for any loss or damage alleged to be caused directly or indirectly by the advice contained herein.

ISBN: 1532736681
ISBN 13: 9781532736681
Library of Congress Control Number: 2016906190
CreateSpace Independent Publishing Platform
North Charleston, South Carolina

Dedication

This book is dedicated to all the professionals, past, present, and future, the human capital of the business world. This is for those of you who have goals and ambition but haven't got the guidance you deserved. This is for those of you who have the courage to stand up, in spite of the obstacles, keep it moving forward and to do what other's don't - succeed.

Table of Contents

Introduction · ix

Chapter 1 It's Not About SMART Goals – It's About Being Smart With Your Goals · 1
Chapter 2 Making Your Professional Network Work for You · · · · 25
Chapter 3 Your Words Have Meaning – Communicate for Success · 49
Chapter 4 When Discussing Your Career, It's All About Framing and Positioning. · · · · · · · · · · · · · · · · 73
Chapter 5 Make Your Agenda *the* Agenda for Your Career Development · 97
Chapter 6 From Mentoring to Sponsorship, Cultivate the Right Relationship for Your Success · · · · · · · · · · · 118
Chapter 7 Leadership – What's It to You? · · · · · · · · · · · · · · · · · 142

Acknowledgements · 165
About the Authors · 167
About the Authors · 169

Introduction

Welcome to achieving your career success.

What this book is not about: This book is not about theory or concept. It's not a book of great ideas that only succeed under ideal conditions.

What this book is about: This book is about you *while* you're in your job and how to successfully navigate everyday.

There are so many books out there that tell you a number of important things: how to land a job, how to change jobs, and to how to switch careers. We wrote this book, the first in our series, because we recognize the importance of the skills and daily behaviors that all professionals should master to achieve their career goals.

We're not going to make this complicated. In fact, it's easier than you think. The insights, tips, questions, and words of caution were gleaned from our years of real-world corporate and entrepreneurial experiences. The good, the bad, the ugly, and all the stuff your boss and the organization don't want you to know. We're going to make this real and practical.

Originally, we planned to have a detailed introduction for you. But we know you don't have time for that.

So let's get to it.

Much love – and here's to your success,

Francine & Dolores

One

It's Not About SMART Goals – It's About Being Smart With Your Goals

IT'S NOT ABOUT SMART GOALS – IT'S ABOUT BEING *SMART* WITH YOUR GOALS.

Setting goals is the key to success. Goals are so important it's hard to imagine not having them.

Career goals are more than just specific goals. They may include time frames, financial milestones, or specific behaviors in which you want to engage. Being clear about your career goals is a professional imperative. It's easy to get caught up in the day-to-day routines and lose sight of your goals, eventually having a career by default. You may earn the money, if you're fortunate, but without the career you want. This is why goals are so important. Too often people wake up mid-career and realize, earnings or not, they simply aren't happy.

Clarity on what your goals are and the outcomes of achieving them is key. This chapter will guide you through the essential process of setting your goals and making them a reality. One of the most important aspects of career goal achievement is always keeping your goals in mind. Again, this chapter will help you ensure that happens, regardless of what else is going on for you.

Getting clear on your career goals and how to achieve them through specific behaviors is where the most successful people are focused. How you talk about your goals and with whom you discuss them is another method for achieving them. We're talking about being *smart* with your goals, and that means creating a strategy to make them happen.

Being smart with your goals also means recognizing when you are considering a larger goal versus a smaller one. When you're thinking about that next big promotion – a larger goal, to be -you must also consider how to accomplish the smaller goals to make that happen. Those smaller goals necessitate finding out who you need to know, what you need to know, and what behaviors you need to engage in.

Big careers don't just happen. They are planned. Getting clear on your goals and developing a strategy to achieve them is how it gets done.

Ready? Good – let's get started.

DON'T JUST MAKE AN EFFORT – MAKE THE RIGHT EFFORT.
Goal achievement can be challenging. You have professional goals that require specific efforts. Knowing what efforts you need to make in a changing environment also is challenging. If your organization hasn't offered clear objectives for you to execute and you find that you're accomplishing little in the way of getting closer to your goal, then it's time to strategize. Take inventory of what gets you positive attention, notice when your efforts yield the results you want (and when they don't), and notice how much time you're spending on these efforts. Your goals are why you're here; being crystal-clear on what they are matters, but being crystal-clear on what to do about them is equally important.

Have any of the individuals in my organization actually helped me achieve my goals or desired outcomes?

BE CRYSTAL-CLEAR WHEN DESCRIBING YOUR PROFESSIONAL GOALS.

One requirement for success is communicating your goals to decision makers in a way that makes them not only want to help you but also feel confident in providing support. This is priority #1. Lack of clarity hinders your progress. Not thinking about what you are trying to achieve and poor communication of your goals limits those in your organization who could otherwise help position you for professional success.

Should you be able to do something on your own, maybe, but that doesn't mean you should shun assistance or deny yourself access to resources if it helps you achieve your goal.

YOUR NETWORK IS A GOAL.

Ensure you fully understand what you are trying to accomplish when thinking about connecting with others who can help you in your career. Ask yourself the following question: "What do I want from my network?"

As you progress through your professional goals, you'll find that you'll need to rely on those in your network from time to time. The goal of developing a robust network follows a similar execution strategy as any other professional goal does. It's important to know the purpose of connecting with others; it lays the foundation for all of your interactions at work, events, and conferences.

HAVE I REALLY DONE THE DUE DILIGENCE IN THE AREA THAT I AM INTERESTED IN PURSUING?

Many of us have a great idea or a passion for something. And if we're being truthful with ourselves, some of us would have pursued different career paths as well. But passion is one thing, and reality is another. Striving to have both is awesome! But what you may want to do doesn't always translate into a successful career or business opportunity.

Make sure you truly know and understand the profession you are pursuing. Is the field already crowded? Do you have a niche idea or a "me too" one? What will it take for you to be known in that particular area? Are you prepared to endure the length of time that it may take to build a business? At a minimum, know what it takes and what you are willing to do to get there. Only after you've completed this task can you create executable strategies.

UNDERSTAND WHAT YOU ARE TRYING TO ACHIEVE.

What is/are your goal(s)? This may sound like a simple question, but it can be quite challenging to answer. Oftentimes, people conflate their goals with their desired outcomes or miss the prerequisite goals that must be achieved before tackling the big goal. For example, you want that director position that you know will open in six months. The big goal is the position, of course. It's achieved through the prerequisite goals, such as completing specific projects, closing big sales, or meeting the right person who can recommend you for the position. It's in reaching the big goal (director position) that other outcomes are experienced. In terms of your career, that might mean access to important people or generally just getting into "the right room." Being clear on the outcomes of achieving the big goal and what each prerequisite goal is allows for a greater probability of success.

Many people offer great advice, some of it quite valuable. But your path is your own, so don't grab onto everything just because it sounds good or worked for someone else.

TALK TO THOSE WITH WHOM YOU DON'T NORMALLY INTERACT WHENEVER THE OPPORTUNITY PRESENTS ITSELF.

You can call this "crossing Org Chart boundaries." For example, don't engage those who you already know or work closely with at large meetings or events. Use these opportunities to talk to someone with whom you normally don't connect or would need a formal or scheduled meeting to talk to. Take a chance – introduce yourself to that person. What a great opportunity to request a meeting with that individual and continue the conversation. Such dialogue requires no commitment from either of you but provides an opportunity to introduce yourself and your goals. Don't forget: Often, many things that happen related to work don't happen in formal settings, so maximize the opportunity. Position yourself.

THE DEPARTURE – USE IT TO ACHIEVE YOUR GOALS.

The simplest action that you can do is say "Thanks," "It was great to meet/know you," "Let's stay in touch" – then do it. Take the opportunity to commit to following up with important people. Get a next step on the calendar. Just because you're leaving an event – or even a company – doesn't mean you're finished with your colleagues. When looking ahead, it's easy to say goodbye and never look back. However, you never know where your contacts and former contacts may end up. Ensure that at the end of your interaction, the manner in which you depart still speaks to the goals you want to achieve.

THINK LIKE YOU'RE ALREADY A SUCCESS.

Who you believe you are shows up quite prominently. Presenting yourself in a light that demonstrates your worth (not necessarily where you are currently) is part of a success-based identity. For example, if you have expertise but are not currently in a position where you utilize it, create a business card that advertises this rather than your current job title.

When creating your plan, include the specific way you intend to execute each step.

CREATE A STRATEGY THAT INCLUDES MORE THAN THE OUTCOME YOU DESIRE.

You must be strategic in deciding how you want to show the world who you are; this may include appearance, communication style, and where you physically go to meet decision makers. Strategic planning also includes the execution of the process. A great plan can go awry easily because of poor execution. Keep the goal in mind every time and every place you show up.

FORGET THE EXPERTS. IF ALL ROADS LEAD TO ROME, TRAVEL THE ONE THAT INTERESTS YOU.

There is a lot of advice about how to succeed in any endeavor. Some of it will be useful for you, but some of it won't. Everyone has their own path, and for some people it's more efficient than for others. Your path might be bumpy or smooth, short or meandering. It doesn't matter. As long as it's authentic, success will follow. Clarifying your time frame and what you can manage are the main considerations when choosing your path.

Generally speaking, you can follow in others' footsteps and you'll get to the finish line, but they still got there first. Authentic success means reaching the finish line that's been set up just for you. Understanding what you're willing and able to do is part of the strategy for success.

ALWAYS USE ACHIEVEMENT-ORIENTED LANGUAGE WHEN DESCRIBING YOUR GOALS. ACCOMPLISHMENTS ARE MEASURABLE, BUT AVOIDANCE TACTICS ARE NOT.

This advice is incredibly valuable and easily overlooked. Generally, people use both positive and negative language when expressing their goals. They spell out what they are striving to achieve and then remind themselves of what they're trying to avoid. But here's the truth: You already know what you don't want, so you don't have to verbalize it. Declaring in clear, achievement-oriented language what you *do* want to achieve helps determine the milestones you need to reach and other tracking measures to ensure you're on the right path. The greatest value of achievement-oriented language lies in your ability to create an outcome assessment. This cannot be done with avoidance language; when you avoid an outcome, it's only temporary (you have to plan to avoid the outcome every day), whereas, once you achieve a goal, you can move on to the next goal, and the previous achievement cannot be taken away from you.

IT ISN'T ABOUT SMART GOALS – IT'S ABOUT *BEING SMART WITH YOUR GOALS.*

Some goals may be related but require the completion of one goal in order to focus on the next. If you've ever had to write a business plan, you'll recall that there are quite a number of considerations to be made, from market conditions to competition to pricing structure and the order in which certain activities must be executed. For example, you wouldn't try to get funding without having the business plan completed. Similarly, whether you are planning your next career move or becoming an entrepreneur, the larger goal of success in these endeavors requires a multitude of smaller achievements that need prioritization. Clarity on what those achievements are and a strategy for each allow you stay focused so you can achieve success. There is no need to try to boil the ocean. While you certainly want to achieve all that you've set out to do, being smart with your goals means knowing when and under what conditions certain steps are taken.

USE SOCIAL MEDIA STRATEGICALLY.

This is a goal-focused behavior – diverging from that path could be disastrous. Almost everyone uses some form of social media, from Facebook to Instagram to LinkedIn, just to name a few. Some of these social media platforms are personal and should be a place where you can be your most expressive without consequence. But we all know that nothing could be further from the truth. In our hyper-connected world, it's easy to forget that you might be connected to someone who simply does not have your best interests at heart. Remaining goal focused on social media platforms includes not just what you say or post but who you interact with and how you interact with them. Sure, you can't control who follows you, but you can absolutely control your choices of whom you follow. These groups or individuals should be heavily geared toward your professional goals.

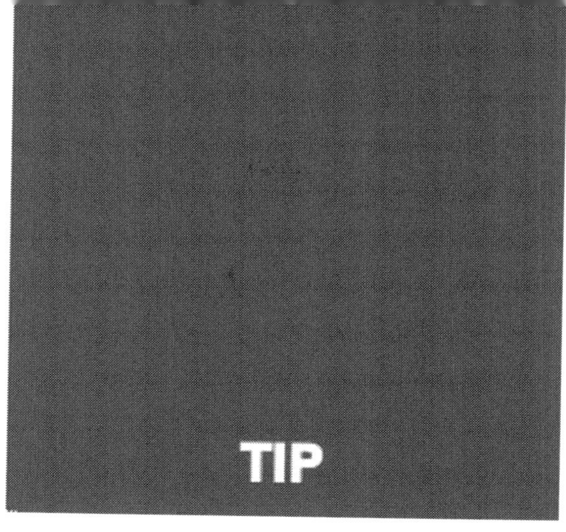

If you're just starting out in your career, take an inventory of all the places you show up on social media. You may have to delete an account or two and start over.

DON'T GET ABSORBED INTO OTHERS' GOALS.

You have your goals and others have theirs. It may appear at times that by helping others achieve their goal you will get where you want to go. But it's easy to get sucked into doing something for someone who never serves your greater goal. Of course, there are people who you'll want to help from time to time, be they family, other colleagues, or friends. There is nothing inherently wrong with helping others, but if it gets in the way of working on your own goals, it doesn't help you. Keeping your goals in mind, recognizing when doing a favor will help, hurt, or delay your goal is imperative.

In addition, it's important to note how helping that person will reflect on you professionally. Will getting involved in someone else's goal affect your personal branding to the degree that your professional identity is lost on your audience? For example, if your good friend wants to open a coffee shop and needs some help, but you've got your eyes on the C-suite in your company, it's essential you stay mindful of how this will reflect on you insofar as others you meet will make a determination regarding who you are and what you're capable of.

NOTES

NOTES

Two

Making Your Professional Network Work for You

MAKING YOUR NETWORK WORK FOR YOU.

It is very nice to know a lot of people or say that you have a large network of connected individuals. However, it is more important that you are clear on why you have this network and how you can leverage it effectively for your professional success.

Building your network is about having the right people resources to complement your skills to assist you in achieving your goals. Also, it is about you becoming known as an invaluable resource to others.

Understanding your network's purpose often starts with having a solid network plan. Planning what you want your network to look like (not just names and titles of individuals) creates a network that ultimately works for you. Don't lose your way by forgetting your desired end results, which is easy to do. Start at the end and work your way backward. Envision what you want your network to look like when all is said and done. Then go build it.

When you go out and network, be purposeful. Have your offering ready to share. Why? To engage the individuals that you want in your network. Also, you are positioning yourself as knowledgeable and valuable. Know what you are going to say when you meet them. Go beyond telling them just about what you do for your organization. Think of something unique about yourself to share that is memorable.

Last, but not least, follow up. This is paramount, and we don't do enough of it. Maintaining your network will be challenging at times, but is often what sets you and others apart. Set up routines that keep your network apprised of your actions. Be aware of what they are doing as well. This will pay off tremendously.

No one said creating the right professional network was easy. It doesn't just happen overnight; it is often incremental. However, once you create a network that helps you achieve your professional goals and become deliberate in your actions with your network, you will be set up for long-term career success.

Now turn the page and learn additional insights and information to create a network that works for you – even when you don't know it!

YOUR NETWORK GOALS HAVE A PURPOSE.

Ask yourself, "What am I trying to achieve with this goal?" If you cannot answer that question, rethink your goal. You should be crystal-clear on why the goal is important to you and what it will help you achieve as you build your network. This is often one of the major pitfalls in maintaining a robust network. We don't think about what the goal will help us accomplish; we jump right into the action only to wonder later why we didn't accomplish the goal we set.

Has anything changed in my professional or personal life that requires me to have a new or different network?

FOCUS EARLY ON THE OUTCOMES THAT YOU WANT TO ACHIEVE AS YOU BUILD YOUR NETWORK.

Many of us spend time on who is in our network, the size of our network, and what our network can do for us. But it's more important to think about the outcomes you want and build a network that comprises individuals to support you in achieving those results. Just having a network of connections that serves no purpose (except that you know one another) will neither currently nor later aide you in your professional success.

DO I REALLY KNOW WHAT MY CURRENT NETWORK IS CAPABLE OF HELPING ME ACHIEVE?

Sometimes this is the toughest step – taking inventory of your network, determining the value of it and doing something about it. You cannot treat everyone in your network as an equal. Even tougher is determining who those individuals are and what actions you need to take. Some individuals in your network serve little to no value in terms of reaching your current goals. Then there are others who provide great value.

You must decide how much time and effort you want to spend on each type of relationship. The important part is recognizing the challenge – and doing something about it.

FOCUS, FOCUS, FOCUS.

A great rule of thumb is deciding on a maximum of three people to whom you plan to introduce yourself at a meeting or event. Hopefully you have done your homework beforehand on those three people. Once you arrive, pay attention to name tags. We often don't think about the importance of name tags; we usually forget the names anyway. However, since you have strategically thought beforehand whom you would like to meet, name tags become invaluable pieces of information. Name tags allow you to seek your intended connection. If that person is the speaker or a panel member, don't waste your time standing in the long line of people to introduce yourself. Unless you have something earthshaking to share, the person probably won't remember you later. However, if you must stand in line, use it as an opportunity to acknowledge that there are many others waiting; it's crowded and you would just like to ask the person to follow up later on. It's more than likely that the person won't say no; in fact, he or she will probably volunteer the best way to contact them. If the person doesn't, just ask. More importantly, spend your time connecting with those in the room you planned to meet in the first place – one of the major reasons that you are there.

Attend events that provide you with an opportunity that you would not get otherwise or elsewhere.

YOU ARE ONLY AS GOOD AS YOUR WORD.

Why do you take a person's business card if you have no intention of following up? Why do you give your business card if you don't want to? Just because everyone is trading cards doesn't mean you have to as well. It's easy to be graceful about it, so stop handing out your cards to anyone and everyone. Also, stop asking for them if you have no intention of following up. If people really need your contact information, provide them with your email address. If someone is truly interested in connecting with you again, he or she will follow up. Most don't. Once again, focus on those three individuals: You want to network with them, not only to give your card but also to obtain theirs and follow up later.

NO WORK CONTACT IS A BAD CONTACT.

You don't have to go through your professional life (or personal, for that matter) developing deep, meaningful relationships with everyone. Our lives at work are not geared toward that end; time is always a factor, and let's not forget that the organization is expecting you to deliver results. There will be some deep relationships that you develop and many that you won't. In your network, it's okay to have loose connections. But figure out which ones should be loose and which should be deep. Consciously decide to what degree you want to engage with certain members in your network; don't leave it to chance.

MAKE YOUR PROFESSIONAL NETWORK DIVERSE – KEEP YOURSELF CONNECTED TO MULTIPLE GROUPS AND OUTLETS.

Many of us work for great organizations, and many of us work for some that are not so great. Either way, we spend a lot of time at work, and it has a way of absorbing us. It sometimes becomes a situation in which our network comprises only individuals whom we see at work. Such a situation can be disastrous, especially if something changes, like the loss of a job, the need or desire to get another job, or changing professions. Your professional network should comprise people with whom you work, those with the same professional interests as you but who are outside of your company, and groups that you have a pure interest in being a part of for your personal self-development.

Once again, the time to develop your network is not when you need it; build it from the beginning over time. It's difficult to develop your career and your network simultaneously, but it's a reality, and it pays off. If you already haven't yet started your network, now is the time!

Don't let your network stagnate. Add individuals over time and vary your choices so you're not including the same types of individuals, professions, or groups that you have had in your network for years.

EVALUATE YOUR SOCIAL CAPITAL.

Now review the actual people in your network and the groups to which you belong. Are they similar to you in terms of profession, age, gender, ethnicity, or experiences? Or are they individuals from different backgrounds who have diverse experiences and various connections? You have to decide what is best for you in achieving your goals; however, having a diverse network (versus one in which everyone has similar experiences and connections) tends to pay off for obvious reasons. Ensure that your professional network is diversified.

DON'T TALK JUST TO THE CONFERENCE PARTICIPANTS.
Many people make a conference a success; some are more obvious in their efforts than others. Take the time to observe the individuals who are less obvious. Watch their interactions and what they do. They are often great resources of information and knowledge, and often serve as gatekeepers to those you may want to network with. Leverage their expertise and connections to assist you; never underestimate their power and influence. Talk to them and share what you are trying to achieve.

UNDERSTAND THE PURPOSE OF YOUR NETWORK.

What do you want your network to help you achieve? It's nice to know a lot of people or say that you are connected with a lot of individuals, but it is important that, based on your goals, you are clear on why you have the network you have and how it enables you to achieve your clearly stated goals.

The ultimate professional network to have is a group of professionals who support and sponsor your goals without you asking (of their own accord) because they know what you are trying to achieve and want to ensure your success.

DECIDE ON WHAT YOU OFFER YOUR NETWORK.
What do you offer (skills, introductions, expertise, etc.) that your network would deem important or useful? We often think about what a network can help us achieve, but it is just as important to think about what one "brings to the table" and to be open about it. Being known as a person with a certain skill or ability is not only viewed as helpful but also appreciated. Such giving pays off in tremendous dividends.

SHARE YOUR SOCIAL CAPITAL – AND BE SERIOUS ABOUT IT.
Be ready to offer your connections. Even though you've sought out a particular person, you have connections just as they do. Offer yours as well, and not just any list of names but rather individuals who are willing to assist on your behalf for that person, if asked. Dropping names adds no value to you or the person with whom you are speaking. If anything, it can backfire if you're not careful; the world is small, so make sure that you know the people you actually say you know. And be knowledgeable enough about them and their skills and/or connections.

JOIN PROFESSIONAL GROUPS.

To become known in your organization, join one of the professional networks within your company. Seek projects for which you can volunteer; position yourself for others to see you contributing and in action. Don't forget about external professional networks, either. They can help those outside of your organization know about you and your work.

FIND PARTNERS, SUPPORTERS, COLLABORATORS AND CHEERLEADERS FOR YOUR CAREER.

Nobody does it alone. Similar to building a network that works for you, this also includes non-career-related collaborators. A support network of other professionals, colleagues, or friends can help keep you on track and lift you up if you experience a setback. Choose this group wisely and share appropriately.

BUILD A NETWORK BY CREATING BUY-IN WITH YOUR GOALS. This is a challenge for many. Your goals are uniquely important to you, and "selling" others on them requires a clear strategy. Generally speaking, being passionate about what you want to achieve and projecting that passion plays a significant role. In addition, clarity on how reaching your goals will help the organization (or your customers or investors) goes a long way toward creating buy-in. Let's face it – altruism only goes so far. It's true that your investors and leaders want you to succeed, not only because it's nice, but also because they benefit from your success in some way. Developing a strategy to communicate the projected benefits of your success demonstrates a win-win for everyone.

NOTES

NOTES

Three

Your Words Have Meaning – Communicate for Success

YOUR WORDS HAVE MEANING.

Kind of a no-brainer, right? But this is your career we're talking about, not everyday conversation. Effective communication means pretty much what it sounds like. Being an effective communicator is how others understand what you want or need. Effective communication in your career is even more particular.

This chapter will help guide you through some of the ways to connect with important decision makers, peers and superiors so that you can set your career on the right path. Effective communication includes the specific words you choose, with whom you use them, your attitude when you speak (both verbal and physical), as well as how you follow up. More importantly, it means effectively asking for what you want and state why you should get it.

Communication, of course, is a two-way street. Successfully navigating the world of effective communications for your career success means listening to others. This, we know, can be difficult at times. The tips and insights in this chapter will help you work on receiving and providing feedback, both great opportunities to practice effectiveness.

Finally, in addition to words, you must be clear in your meaning. Successful effective communication gives others insights into your thought process. What information do you want other people to have about you? Do you want to communicate that you're a problem solver? A great coach to peers and subordinates? Excellent at defusing conflict? This chapter will also provide insights, tips and things to watch out for to ensure that you can do all of these things effectively.

Okay, enough talk – let's get communicating!

Effective communication also includes how you communicate your attitude. Ask yourself, "Does my body language communicate my professionalism and my career goals?"

STRATEGIZE ABOUT HOW YOU COMMUNICATE ABOUT *YOU*. Think about the message you want to communicate to individuals in your organization about you and/or your skills. Decide what they should know and how they should know it. For example, you may find a project in your organization requiring a specific skill that you have. Here's what you do: Find the person or group working on that project. Introduce yourself. Take some time to get to know them and initially share what you are currently working on. Once you have more information about this person or group and their work, offer assistance to let them know of your interest. Just be savvy before jumping into any conversation about what you can offer early on; you probably don't know the person, and he or she doesn't know you either, so think about how to present yourself. Remember: What you communicate about *you* sends many messages, whether intention or unintentional.

MAKE YOUR CONVERSATIONS COUNT, NO MATTER THE SITUATION.

How you start one conversation can often lead to many others. You naturally engage in casual conversations, whether in a meeting, at an event, or during a conference. Often you start with one person, and that person connects you with another person or resource and so on. Many of these conversations will be brief in nature, since time is usually scarce. So maximize that time by sharing what you are trying to achieve up front. Acknowledge that neither of you have a lot of time, and then get your point across quickly but effectively. Ask if the person has any ideas or know someone to recommend that you talk to. In return, always ask if there is anything that you can provide. If you make such conversations meaningful, then over time you have in your arsenal people, ideas, or resources to share with others, which can make many others want to have meaningful conversations with you! Always ensure that what you share with others is meaningful and real.

KNOWING WHO YOU ARE TALKING TO CAN PAY OFF.

Planning effective communication with others is paramount. We often take for granted the importance of really knowing those with whom we interact. Especially when at work, we often rely on organizational charts and titles, which can help, but at times they don't tell the whole story about the individual. Always do your homework when reaching out to people in your organization whom you don't know or know a little about. You may have an opportunity to meet people with whom you've wanted to speak for some time; perhaps they could assist you with your career. Knowing something about them shows your interest in them and what they do. You may even be able to share something about you and how it intersects with what you know about them. This will clearly demonstrate that you're genuinely interested in them or their work and aren't wasting their time. In return, they will be more willing to assist you.

There is nothing wrong with a little Internet sleuthing, like using LinkedIn or another public profile. Just be sure of what you are looking for, and that finding it will give you the insight you need for the purposes of the conversation you want to have.

BE CONSISTENT: SELECT ONE THING THAT YOU WANT TO SHARE.

No matter what work-related event you attend, have at least one thing that you are prepared to discuss or want others to know. Everyone will then have one unfailing story about you. Do you want to share something that relates to you in preparation for something else, like a new project coming your way? Is there something that you want to remind others of? Maybe you have a success story to share or a partnership that was a success. Create and share your consistent message; you will then have a better chance of being remembered.

COMMUNICATE WHAT YOU ARE TRYING TO ACHIEVE. Often we think that we must have a long, engaging conversation and then get to your goal. Yes, this isn't the first thing someone wants to hear, and tact is important. But share what your goals are. For example, if you are attending a professional work conference and have a goal of meeting certain leaders who have job openings, then communicate your interest in a tactful manner. Tell them that you want to learn more about their function and how a background such as yours could fit into their group. If not, what would they recommend you do? Are you working on something that you've received great feedback on and think would be relevant to their team? Ask to share the project and the lessons you learned over a cup of coffee or tea later because you'd like to get their feedback.

These are just a few ideas; there are multiple approaches to this conversation, if you're creative. However, before you share anything, give some robust thought to what your goals are before you communicate them to anyone.

CLOSE THE CONVERSATION WITH MEANINGFUL FOLLOW-UP. Once you engage someone, you now own following up with them. This can be as simple as a "thank you" at the end of the chat or scheduling the next meeting. Think about what would make someone want to connect with you beyond that initial meeting. Many times, it is something that you offer, that you know that you can do, or a skill that you have. Create an inventory of things you can offer before your next meeting. Then, as you listen to the other person, see if you can mention something that you do well. This is not offering to help them; it's simply sharing. Wait to offer this once you really understand what the person needs – hopefully at your next meeting.

Practice important conversations with others who will provide you with valuable feedback.

YOU ARE YOUR OWN MARKETING PRODUCT. SELL, SELL, SELL.
It's important to develop a vocabulary that supports your goals when you speak to others about your ambitions. Using passionate language to demonstrate your career desires is a communication skill worth developing. Whether you're speaking to your supervisor or a higher-level colleague, it's essential that, when you make your desires known, you also clarify why you are capable of achieving goals and why you are the person to hire/promote.

TAILOR YOUR LANGUAGE AND COMMUNICATIONS TO HIGHLIGHT WHAT YOU WANT TO ACHIEVE.

Knowing your audience, what's important to them and what you want to communicate to them is key. Make every attempt to discover what is important to the people with whom you're speaking. If what's important to you is not aligned with what they find important in terms of career development, find a common ground and start the conversation there. You're more likely to achieve buy-in and support over time when others feel a connection to your goals, even if they didn't have one originally.

USING FEEDBACK FOR GROWTH.

Feedback is an important part of professional development. Leadership track managers use feedback to learn and grow. The ability to accept critique and uncomfortable feedback is a key quality of future and current leaders. Pay attention to the experience of receiving feedback, even from a superior who provides feedback poorly. Asking questions for clarification sends the message that you want to grow and succeed; offering defenses without being asked to do so might have the opposite effect. Listen for the nugget of truth and use it to achieve your goal.

When communicating with others about what you hope they can do for you, be direct while asking. For some, being direct may equate to voicing an inappropriate expectation. Know who you are speaking with and how they respond to various styles of direct communication.

COMMUNICATION WORKS BEST WHEN IT'S CLEAR AND DIRECT. You have career goals, and you're going to want to talk about them. Now that you are in front of the right person, how are you going to communicate them? This is not the time to drop hints or leave the door open for a later time – you may not have a second opportunity. Clearly articulating your career desires and clearly stating how this person can help may increase your chances of success. This isn't about shameless self-promotion. This is a conversation with those who can help you reach your goals. The clearer you are, the more they understand, and if they are not in a position to help, they may offer a resource that can. This can only happen when you know what you want to say and then you say it.

YOU CAN'T BE EVERYONE'S FRIEND.

It's true – you can't. That doesn't mean you don't speak to everyone as if they are important, from the bathroom cleaner to your highest superior to the stranger in the lobby. How you speak to others is another way of communicating who you are and your value to the organization. You may not be inviting your manager or coworkers to holiday dinners, but your tone, the words you choose and your body language are forms of communication that alerts people to your attitude. Honesty, clarity and diplomacy should be your first go-to skills when communicating with anyone and everyone.

BE CLEAR WITH DECISION MAKERS.

You have a plan and a strategy to succeed in your career. This means communicating with various people about your goals. In addition, it also means being heard in general, whether in team meetings or during a private conversation with a superior. This is not a time to be shy. Being assertive requires that you speak up. Stating your goals or desires in a concrete manner, being clear and being direct are the only ways. If you find yourself raising your voice an octave higher to end a statement, it then sounds like a question, and you'll have difficulty gaining buy-in or understanding. For example, there is a project you want to lead; it's challenging, it will highlight your skills and successful completion will impress all the right people. Make a clear statement as to the reason you want this project and what its success will do for you and the organization. If your statement sounds like you're asking permission rather than presenting your case, you might not like the answer. Be clear, be direct and use concrete statements. Be sure to highlight the skill set you'll be leveraging and be clear as to why it's of value. As mentioned earlier, always know your audience, but also say what you mean.

If you find yourself saying or almost saying, "I don't mean to sound mean or offensive," it's a good bet you're about to be offensive. Effective communication requires thoughtful and meaningful word choice to get your point across.

FEEDBACK IS A SKILL.

Providing feedback to others is a communication skill that takes practice. The purpose of providing feedback is to let people you are communicating with know how they are doing. If you are speaking to superiors, this might be in the form of alerting them to what you need in terms of support or development. When providing feedback to peers and subordinates, clarity is key. Framing feedback in positive language is a solutions-focused way to provide guidance and feedback at the same time. For example, if you're working on a team and you need to alert team members that their efforts are not yielding the necessary results, you can offer an alternative while also providing honest feedback. Feedback is a tool meant to help or improve an individual or a situation. Use it for these purposes, and you'll see results.

LISTENING IS A SUPERPOWER.

This may sound obvious, but at the same time this can be a challenge, especially if you have a lot to share. For example, in a team meeting, suppose you have a great idea or an important observation to make or a great solution to a tricky problem. Chances are, other people in the room believe the same thing. They may all be wrong and only you are correct. But you have to sit there and listen to them speak and offer ideas that are not executable, among other problems. You want to jump in and just say what needs to be said and move this meeting along. Instead of listening, you're focusing on what you want to say because you're sure it's so much better.

Keeping an open ear is essential and an especially savvy communication skill. It allows you to gain insight into others' thinking, learning what's important to them and how they view and solve problems. Framing your conversations around what others feel is important can help you gain buy-in for getting what you need to achieve success in the organization.

STAY POSITIVE.

Negative and unpleasant experiences abound in almost any undertaking. During your career, you'll meet many people, from your coworkers to executive leaders. People will ask you what you think, and you'll want to answer immediately – but stop! Choose your words carefully. Framing a discussion around words that demonstrate intentional action versus negativity is good practice. For example, you're about to provide feedback or an opinion about a project. You have noticed something is missing from the planning. Before pointing that out, be sure to have a solution. Making a negative statement or a critique about those involved and letting that hang there without any ideas to remedy the situation will not have a desirable impact. Reframe your ideas using positive language. This shows that your intention is continued improvement rather than being the person who's always mired in negativity. Positive language communicates to others that you can be accountable and a problem solver.

NOTES

NOTES

Four

When Discussing Your Career, It's All About Framing and Positioning.

IT'S ALL ABOUT FRAMING AND POSITIONING.

You ultimately own your career and the discussions that come along with it. It is important not to let anyone take that away from you. You are the only one who really knows or should know what is important to you related to your professional career and aspirations.

Obviously, you have supporters and partners, as you can't create or maintain a successful career alone. How you engage and connect with them to discuss your career is important. This means having the right career discussions about your career in the present and for the future.

This also means taking the necessary time to manage such conversations, just as you do for other aspects of your job. We often take for granted the importance of sitting down with our managers and really delving into what will make us successful in the long run. Don't be lulled into a performance discussion masked as a career discussion or a list of training classes your manager thinks you need to take as a robust career discussion.

If a career discussion is occurring several times throughout the year, the likelihood of the above happening is slim. Such ongoing dialogue helps you and your manager to always be on top of what you aspire to do and what the organization is supportive of you doing. It is a two-way street.

More importantly, an ongoing discussion ensures that you and your manager are prepared to discuss your aspirations and potential career moves when asked by others in your company at a moment's notice. Remember, there are others who may not have direct management oversight accountability for you but who serve just as important a role in your development; they need to know about you as well, such as your leader's manager or someone else in another part of your company.

So take nothing for granted. Plan your career discussions and learn who, beyond your direct manager, knows about you and what you aspire to achieve. It is important that as many people as possible are aligned to you, which often starts with ongoing conversations. As you grow and evolve in your career, so does the need for ongoing career conversations.

The next several pages of this chapter will help you have the career conversations needed to serve as a catalyst for the right actions in your career success.

"THIS IS A HUGE OPPORTUNITY. HOW CAN I STAY CONNECTED TO THE ORGANIZATION AND THE LEADERS SO THEY SEE THE WORK THAT I'M DOING?"

Just because you have a big job or role does not mean that anyone will be paying attention – unless you screw it up. I've worked in some remote locations with big assignments, and it is tough staying top of mind. If you are successful, it's more than likely that you got stuff done. You made things happen seamlessly.

Well, don't let it be so seamless that you are forgotten. Hold your leadership accountable for ensuring they pay attention to you; they need to know about the work that you are doing as well what you are capable of doing. This is where your professional network becomes important and invaluable. Also, make sure that more than one person is talking about you at the right time and in the right conversations. Don't leave it all up to your manager.

Making time to speak with your leaders about your career outside of the annual or biannual review process is a goal. Have an agenda ready. Know what you want to say, be focused and develop ideas for your achievement. In other words, be prepared.

DON'T WAIT FOR THE ORGANIZATION TO COME TO YOU.

We often wait until that certain time of year when the organization gives us official permission to speak to our management about our career. That particular time is important; in many organizations, such action wouldn't occur if a dedicated time didn't exist. Make it a part of your ongoing review and talk with your manager as well as others in your company or network. This is no different from the goals you have committed to accomplishing for the organization this year. Many of us are comfortable discussing how we are continually progressing toward our goals and objectives, such as in our monthly updates or meetings. We need to have that same level of comfort with our development plans as well. Sometimes, waiting for a specific time to have such a discussion doesn't truly give you the time needed to implement actions or allow you to course correct throughout the year, if needed. At the end of your monthly meetings with your leader, try to specifically talk for 10–15 minutes about your development or career and what you both have committed to do against the progress made to date.

WHERE DO YOU FIT?

Knowing where you fit within your company's talent pipeline at all times is essential to your career growth. It helps you to decide if your current company meets your expectations and if they want to invest in you. You must truly understand if the value of what you offer and your future aspirations are aligned with where the organization sees you headed. Make sure you have more than that once-a-year career discussion. No matter how brief or long the discussion is, it's worth it. If your career discussions are frequent enough, you will get your questions answered. Then you can probe for more details, as you will be better informed. Frequency and an ongoing rhythm helps you, your manager and others aligned to your success avoid career disappointments and surprises that ultimately affect you.

MAKE IT THE RIGHT CONVERSATION BY BEING PREPARED TO DISCUSS WHAT YOU WOULD LIKE TO DO IN YOUR CAREER.

Do your homework beforehand. Don't take a passive role. Clearly articulate what you want. Don't wait for your manager to tell you where the organization sees you going. Do you also see it? Is it really possible within your organization? How long will it take, and what are the real hurdles? Think through the questions you have and try to answer them beforehand to see if they match what your manager says when you meet.

When you didn't get a job or promotion you wanted, have you ever thought of asking your manager or organization not about why you didn't get it but rather what you could do to prepare yourself for next time?

HAVE NOT JUST ONE BUT MULTIPLE CONVERSATIONS WITH THE RIGHT PEOPLE IN YOUR ORGANIZATION IN ADDITION TO YOUR MANAGER.

This is the time to leverage your network and your supporters. I don't believe you can be effective by relying on just one person (your manager) to speak for or about you. Send the message to the organization that you are interested in your career and want to achieve your professional goals. The more individuals who know about you and your career aspirations, the more informed they are when speaking on your behalf. This is especially important if they are in places where you aren't, can't be, or don't know about in your organization.

ASK THE RIGHT QUESTIONS TO UNDERSTAND WHAT YOUR ORGANIZATION IS TRULY PREPARING YOU FOR.

What is the real intention of you moving into that developmental role? What will taking that course help you with, and how will you apply that new skill when you return? How are the things that have been highlighted from a career perspective helping you prepare for the next opportunity? I have seen too many times a lot of "career development" actions that employees engage in and managers support that ultimately lead to nothing. I affectionately call it the "career stall tactic": giving you something to focus on to make you think you are being developed while the organization tries to figure out what to do with you.

AVOIDING THE UNEXPECTED.

You and your manager should be equally prepared for your career discussions at all times. However, often we allow our manager to be in the driver's seat while we act as the passenger when it comes to our careers. Then we are surprised or disappointed when we discover that where we want to go career-wise is not what our manager or the organization has in mind. That surprise or disappointment sometimes leads us to leave our company. What is even more disappointing is that it is usually not our skills that are in question or how we performed on a project or assignment; we are often surprised to hear that it's about a set of expectations that the manager or the organization had of the role that we aspired to, and we had not demonstrated any of the expected behaviors, likely because we simply didn't know about them or that they were required. So going beyond what are the skills needed is paramount.

Ask your manager what the expectations are of the role that you aspire to. Are you expected to drive change, build a culture and engage others in addition to the necessary skills? Are there experiences that you should already have that will differentiate you from others when opportunities arise that you are interested in? Truly understanding the full scope of the opportunities you desire within your company and making this a part of your ongoing career discussions will ensure that you have an equally good chance of choosing the career path you desire. Also, it demonstrates your savvy as it relates to your career. Weave the bigger career picture about you into your career discussions. Remember: You are in control.

DISCUSS AND COMMIT TO ONLY WHAT YOU CAN DELIVER, AND BE TIMELY ABOUT IT.

In our zeal to be seen as helpful or viewed as a valuable resource, we may over-promise or overextend ourselves; then we end up under-delivering. This often goes for the person with whom you are meeting as well: in their zeal to help you, they too may do the exact same thing. But the responsibility lies with you (you asked for the meeting) to ensure that you both know what has been agreed to and when it can be done. At a minimum, this will keep things moving along. Hopefully it will be only the beginning of several more conversations between the two of you.

FINALLY, JUST ENLIST YOUR MANAGER.

Having the conversation with your manager may not be the easiest, whether his or her actions are intentional or unintentional. However, both you and your leaders owe each other to have that professional dialogue. Sometimes it just takes bringing something to someone's attention for a change to occur. Talk to your leaders and let them know of your requests. Enlist them by asking for help with your career, which they should be doing anyway but maybe just need a little help from you.

If only your manager can talk about your performance, accomplishments and professional interests, then you are taking a risk with your career. Make sure that more than one person can speak to your skills and background in your organization.

CONFIRM WHAT YOU ARE BEING PREPARED FOR.

Most of the time, the manager is not ready to answer this, and the employee more than likely doesn't think to ask. Often, career discussions turn to focusing on future training needs or the potential next assignment. That's an easy career conversation. A more robust discussion is one in which you can discuss and clearly link all of the developmental activities that your manager and/or organization has in mind for you. In addition, how is this all preparing you for that next opportunity that you are best suited for? Ask your manager what the developmental work listed in your plan will help you achieve or demonstrate when it is completed. What are the concrete next steps if they are accomplished successfully? Such work should be clearly preparing you for that next assignment, promotion or some critical next move in your career.

When you have the conversation, are you listening carefully to what's being said, or are you listening to respond/defend? Take your time, digest the information and respond accordingly.

KNOW HOW YOUR MANAGER *AND* THE ORGANIZATION WILL YOUR MEASURE SUCCESS.

This is purely about alignment; it has nothing to do with the activity side of development and the tasks that you and your manager have agreed that you will demonstrate. The completion of all of the identified "to dos" in your developmental plan by a certain time doesn't mean that you have successfully mastered them. Know what measures your manager and organization use to determine if you have achieved your development actions successfully. Many times, what is on paper is not often the reality. So ask not only your manager but others early in the process and along the way. Make your career conversations ongoing with those whom you know will have feedback about your development. Hopefully, these individuals give you honest feedback also. Remember: Your manager should not be the only one that you rely on to weigh in on your success.

DETERMINE HOW OTHERS ARE VIEWED AS SUCCESSFUL.
We all know names and titles in our companies. We also know who is viewed as successful. And, obviously, a key indicator is when promotional or even lateral movement occurs. So when such an event happens, use it as an opportunity to learn more by digging a little deeper. Look beyond the career progression of that person, about whom you will undoubtedly read in the announcement. Find out what it really took for that person to get there. The easiest and best way to start is to ask the person directly. Also ask your manager or other leaders in your organization for their perspectives, especially if they know the person. This is even better if such individuals helped that person obtain the career opportunity. If you aspire to reach that level or position, a deeper understanding helps you decide if the role is for you. It also helps you start clarifying what you want and what you'll do to obtain it. By taking such action and then talking to your manager and others, you are signaling your career interest, which makes your career conversations more purposeful and you more prepared.

UNDERSTAND YOUR ORGANIZATION'S PROCESSES.

Learn about your organization's succession or talent management process and where you fit when discussing your career. Most organizations have a designated time in which they review the talent within the organization. Ensure that you not only understand the process but also know where you fit in the process. Do you know who is responsible for discussing you beyond your immediate manager? Probably several people. Make sure you not only understand the process, but where you fit and most importantly what will be said about you.

PUT YOURSELF OUT THERE FOR OTHERS TO SEE YOU IN ACTION.

It is easy just to do our jobs and go home, right? However, if sponsorship and leadership support in your organization are important to you, this means that you'll have to go that extra mile. Ask to take on assignments that will help key leaders in your organization see you in action. How well you perform or complete an assignment often is an indicator to others about your abilities. They will also feel comfortable about approaching you for future opportunities. People are naturally attracted to success and successful individuals. Your leaders are no different.

BEFORE AGREEING TO TAKE THE INTERNATIONAL ASSIGNMENT, HAVE YOUR RETURN TICKET.

Oftentimes, we are so excited about a job opportunity and destination that we forget to ask our manager certain critical questions about what skills or work opportunities the organization feels that the international assignment will provide. Also, ask about your placement or what position you will assume when returning to your home country. Forgetting to ask often leads to returning to a undesirable position or, even worse, no position. It is easy to be forgotten when taking an international assignment and, when you return, nothing has been thought out until your assignment is nearly over. Don't take the position until you have discussed with your manager and others what an international career move means to you and your family if appropriate. Be crystal-clear.

NOTES

NOTES

Five

Make Your Agenda *the* Agenda for Your Career Development

MAKE YOUR AGENDA *THE* AGENDA.

Everyone wants and needs career development. Often, it's your organization that decides what to develop you for. Generally, development takes the form of improvements in your current role. But you have bigger plans, don't you? Of course you want to be successful in your current role, but you also want to move ahead. How can you make that happen? How can you get buy-in and support from your superiors to ensure that you are developed not just for the job you have but also the career you want?

This chapter will offer insights into getting the development you need to move ahead in your career. Make it *your* agenda. Your development must benefit the organization on some level, especially if it's paying for it. But we know that organizations are investing less and less in employee development. You'll have to do some of this stuff on your own – no small feat, but doable if you follow these insights, tips and words of caution, and answer the questions posed.

Career development is more than formal training. A well-rounded development plan includes being mindful of who you are exposed to and how to learn from them. It also includes taking honest inventory of the skills sets you currently possess and being clear on what is needed. You'll see many development programs, training classes, or certificates. Being strategic in your development is necessary for success. Remember, it's your agenda. Chapter 1 talked about setting your goals. Getting the career development you need is part and parcel with that process.

When you are clear on your career goals, then you are clear on the development you need to achieve those goals. They may align with the organization's ideas for your development; sometimes they won't, depending on how the organization works with it's employees. Reaching your development goals, whether they're yours specifically or the organization's, will always benefit you.

"SO HOW DOES THIS POSITION HELP ME REACH MY CAREER OBJECTIVES?"

We tend to focus on what is in front of us right at that moment. If your leader can't articulate this, then this is a warning sign. Don't take a dead-end job. If this is a true assignment to develop you, then the organization should have thought about you and your career steps beyond this one opportunity. It's called succession planning. Make sure there's a plan for you that you want and that your organization supports.

KNOW THE VALUE OF THE ASSIGNMENT YOU ARE TAKING TO YOUR CAREER.

Say you are given a great assignment, and it is the organization's hope that the situation or responsibilities you take on provide you with the right skills to continue to develop. Sometimes this happens; most of the time it doesn't. But either way, know what your organization wants to see that you have demonstrated after completing the assignment. Remember to ask the following: "When this assignment has concluded, what skills will the organization expect me to demonstrate?" Talk about this as you go through the assignment, checking to see if you and the company are aligned at all times. As the assignment moves forward, so should your skills.

DETERMINE YOUR PROFESSIONAL CAPITAL.

How do you communicate your value to your organization? This question may seem odd, but it is actually very important. Shouldn't those you work with or the organization you work in already know this about you? Isn't it why you were hired and what you get paid to do? Don't others see your value in the work you deliver every day? No, not always – and sometimes not at all. Your skills can go totally unnoticed by others in your organization. To be proactive and manage this, take inventory of the skills you bring. Then find out how they align with the skills your organization values. Make this inventory a part of your development plan or career discussions. This helps not only you but also your manager and others in your organization who are aware of your value. Additionally, it will assist you in gaining and practicing new skills you may not have by uncovering any gaps. The more time you take to determine your value and share with others as well as be open to obtaining new skills, the more valuable you become to everyone around you. It is important that you stay on top of your skills, informing others and working on increasing your professional capital.

HAVE I TAKEN THE TIME TO GET THE TRAINING THAT I NEED BEFOREHAND?

You may be saying right now, "I barely have time to get my job done, much less take any courses." Well, if you want to remain competitive with others in your profession (especially if you are entering a new one), getting the appropriate training is essential. Even just having exposure to what you want to do is important; you can get that by attending related courses or training. Also, if what you are currently doing provides you with an opportunity to learn some skills you may want to use later, don't miss out on that. Let it serve both you and your company.

Pay attention to skills that are transferrable. You absolutely want to acquire the skills you need to move up in the company, but also you must be able to use these skills elsewhere. This demonstrates preparation for your future and flexibility.

HOW DO I CURRENTLY LOOK TO THE EXTERNAL WORLD?

Maintaining the necessary skills in your profession is critical in today's world. Even though we no longer stay with companies for extended periods in our careers, this does not mean that it is easy to go from one job to the next or get the type of job that you really want. Don't assume that you will be welcomed with open arms just because you are hired. Often, the real work starts when you are in the job. The skills you exhibit may have worked well in your current organization but may need tweaking elsewhere or – worst-case scenario – you discover they are not relevant anymore. Remember, the longer you stay in one organization, the more you tailor your skills for that company. Always do a quick assessment to see what the market requires against your current skill set for the type of job you have now or desire in the future. If there's a disconnect between the two, then you know what needs to happen: Obtain those needed skills as soon as possible while at your current job, making them a part of your career development plan. This ensures you have a backup plan in case your job or company changes.

ENSURE THE WORK THAT YOU TAKE ON ALIGNS TO THE RIGHT COMPETENCIES YOU NEED FOR YOUR LONG-TERM CAREER GROWTH.

When we start a new job or assignment, usually there is no shortage of work. In fact, there's usually a long list waiting for us, which can often get us sidetracked. Sometimes our given tasks have nothing to do with our job, much less our career. We've all done this, and there are times when such actions are required. However, the issue arises when such activities become the norm. Always ask yourself if an assignment aligns with helping you develop the career skills you need. Don't let it get to a point where you have done what the organization has asked you to do, but it doesn't align to your career plans or prepare you for your next career move. Have the right conversations with your manager and others early on to avoid getting sidetracked.

THINK ABOUT HOW THE ORGANIZATION CAN ACTUALLY SEE YOU IN ACTION.

Many of us shy away from opportunities that let others in the organization see our work or our skills, whether specifically related to our job or not. There is often inherent risk, because if you are successful, everyone sees your success; if you fail, everyone will probably see that as well. Owning your career is often about taking risks. So investigate and pursue opportunities outside of your normal day-to-day tasks that will help advance your career. Yes, you are busy, but your career success is worth it. Is there a professional group in your organization that could provide such an opportunity? Can you demonstrate your readiness to take a leadership role by playing a major role in one of those professional groups? Don't wait for someone to present that great project to you or an opportune time for something to occur – make it happen yourself.

The difference between successful individuals and unsuccessful individuals lies in the formers' willingness to step outside of their comfort zones. Take measured, calculated risks, but take risks nonetheless.

TAKE TIME WITH YOUR DEVELOPMENT PLAN.

We tend to take a lot of time with our goals and objectives. Our development often comes last, if at all. Take just as much time with your development as you do with your goals and objectives. Having the right development plan that includes the right work can pay off. Make sure that you and your manager agree on goals and objectives that will make you visible to others within your organization.

OWN THE BUSINESS OF *YOU*.

Select an area of expertise that you want to be known for in your organization. Ensure that it is a part of what you envision about yourself and your career success. Just like any successful organization, creating a vision statement for your career is a part of your success story. Take the time to create the vision and mission statements about yourself. Where do you see yourself going in the next two to five years? What is your philosophy, and why do you do what you do? What do you desire internally (your vision), and what are the outcomes and impact that you want to have overall (your mission)?

Is there something that you want to be known for in your organization? Then make it your signature so that when something comes up in which your organization needs your level of expertise, you are automatically seen as the expert to help meet the need. Over time, this ensures that others know who you are and may request your leadership.

PEOPLE WILL ALWAYS ASK FOR HELP AND FAVORS. BEFORE YOU SAY YES, ASK YOURSELF, "HOW WILL THIS HELP ME?"
Being helpful is noble and often pays you back. But if helping takes you away from making valuable connections or completing important work, you may need to rethink saying "yes" and strategize more carefully to minimize the impact. Consider what saying "yes" or "no" will cost you. For example, if doing a favor for someone means gaining valuable experience and a new supporter, then it's important to determine how best to make this happen. If saying "no" is the only option in terms of time and money, the other person should understand. In this case, be crystal-clear that it's not something you can do and, if necessary, provide a compelling reason. Learning how to create professional boundaries can help keep you on track for your career development by minimizing detours and distractions.

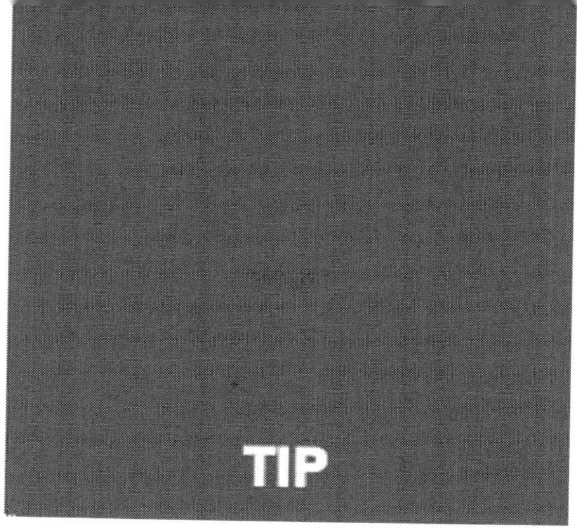

When planning your next career move, include a strategy to hit the three targets.

With every new position or set of responsibilities, a new strategy can be developed.

THREE TARGETS TO HIT WHEN PLANNING YOUR SUCCESS:

- **Access to important people**
- **Development of key skills**
- **Solutions-focused thinking**

These targets are the foundation of your growth and success plan. In fact, part of a Solutions-focused thinking process includes identifying how to gain access to key players and what kind of development will benefit you in that quest. In addition, solutions-focused thinking keeps your eyes on the goals and outcomes you are trying to achieve.

CONSIDER YOUR ROI WITH REGARD TO EDUCATION AND DEVELOPMENT.

Do you need the eMBA, or would some certificates suffice? We love letters after our last names. It denotes expertise, special knowledge, something that makes you stand out. But unless your employer is covering the cost, it can be expensive and time-consuming. In some areas of business, you can get expert training and knowledge through a certificate program rather than advanced degree. Consider the time, energy and financial investment you have to make in a realistic way before deciding. Know what you are truly able to focus on and the rewards for that endeavor – then make it happen.

YOU HAVE A LOT TO DO TO ACCOMPLISH YOUR CAREER GOALS. TAKE SYSTEMATIC INVENTORY OF WHAT YOU HAVE AND WHAT YOU NEED.

Career development can encompass many skills and advanced learning opportunities. It's natural to want to do it all, learn it all and master it all. This can be overwhelming. Prioritize time, energy and finances when deciding what you must do, what you might do and what you can hire or delegate someone else to do. This is a challenging necessity. For each goal you can take inventory of what you already bring to the process, what you might need and even the cost of acquiring it. Being self-sufficient feels great, but this can lead to real burnout and ultimately be counterproductive.

You might have the skills or aptitude for something, but pay attention to the time and energy investment. People often focus on whether they have the skills to do something and lose sight of the time and finances required.

NOTES

NOTES

Six

From Mentoring to Sponsorship, Cultivate the Right Relationship for Your Success

CULTIVATE THE RIGHT RELATIONSHIP FOR YOUR SUCCESS.

Finding someone willing to invest in your career, help you along the way and share their perspective and opinions that you trust isn't easy. But once you find such a person, your relationship becomes invaluable for your ongoing career success. We call this type of relationship *mentoring*.

The quality of mentoring varies in terms of level of commitment, time and support from the person serving as the mentor as well as the individual being mentored. Both parties have to engage equally and actively.

Organizations have mentoring programs that exist in many forms. Some are formal, and many are informal. Some are peer-to-peer, and others are more hierarchal in nature. Senior managers and leaders are paired with certain junior employees based on career needs and/or desires.

Irrespective of the relationship, it is the mentor's responsibility to provide you with feedback, listen to you and help you with your overall career development. It is your responsibility as the mentee to be open and receptive to the feedback.

The highest form of mentoring, sponsorship, provides the above in addition to having someone usually very senior within your company commit to your career advancement and placing his/her reputation – and possibly career – on the line for your benefit. They are banking on your success as a future leader. It is risky for you because you have to be successful.

Going from mentoring to sponsorship if you desire career progression is a smart strategy. However, it doesn't just happen by luck; you have to demonstrate strong performance. In addition, you must understand how your talent management processes work in your organization as well as show that you not only desire to be mentored but are willing to serve as a mentor in return.

But this doesn't guarantee organizational support for your career. It is not just about what you've done but how you position yourself to merit the organization's continued support. This often involves taking risks by raising your hand for certain assignments, letting people know who you are and building strong relationships over time. The time you invest will also show that you value partnering with others to achieve your – and their – career success.

No one has ever been successful on their own when it comes to their career outcomes. If you think about it, no matter what level you are at in your organization, people have helped you get there, whether they coached, gave you feedback or simply watched out for you along the way.

This chapter provides insights and tips that you can use to start or strengthen your mentoring relationships, no matter where you are along your career path. The purpose of mentoring is to help guide and support your career success. Read, share and use this information for your success and helping others who could use your guidance.

SEEK A MENTOR; MORE IMPORTANTLY, A SPONSOR.
Mentors can give you sound advice. But finding those who will put their career on the line and speak on your behalf is paramount. They are called sponsors. Having a relationship with someone of this nature can help you navigate, get noticed and find support.

HAVE A TRACK RECORD OF DEVELOPING OTHERS.

We all know that it is often tough to mentor and coach others. Not for lack of desire; it often comes down to getting our own tasks and projects completed. However, developing yourself is just as important as letting others see that you have the ability to develop your team members. It comes down to taking the time to make this happen. Your mentees need not report to you or be on your team. You can even mentor your peers. The bigger message to the organization is that you are doing your part. The organization and its sponsors will see your actions. If you are successful in mentoring others, you will develop a reputation for it and also demonstrate the value you see in mentoring relationships.

Decide what type of mentoring relationship you want early on before approaching a potential mentor or communicating to your organization your interest.

START WITH THE END IN MIND: DO YOUR HOMEWORK ON THE SPONSORS YOU WANT.

You may know about these people, see their work and level of contribution to the organization. But there's nothing like doing your own due diligence. Find out what others are saying about them. What is their "hallway reputation"? For example, do they have a reputation of ruining careers? You want to know this before you start. You don't want to have to watch your back – you want a quality sponsor. You may have to exit gracefully once you find out the truth.

KNOW SPECIFICALLY WHAT YOU ARE ASKING FOR – AND ASK. In any relationship, it is important to know what you are asking for and also clarify what you can bring to the relationship, especially if you want that that person to serve as a sponsor. You have to know and articulate more than "I would like you to coach me or help me advance in my career." What does that mean? Such a statement can be ambiguous, prompting misaligned expectations. Clarify what you need and want as well as what you can offer. These relationships go both ways. In her book, "Find a Sponsor, The New Way to Fast-Track Your Career," Sylvia Ann Hewlett provides great insight to the responsibilities of a person being sponsored.

BE OPEN AND TRANSPARENT UP FRONT.

If you want the people mentoring you to become sponsors eventually, share that sooner rather than later. If they say that it would be impossible or not preferred, you have a decision to make and/or an action to take. More importantly, from the onset, you aren't surprised, and neither are they. It gives you both a way out or allows the relationship to remain at the level where it started – mentor and mentee.

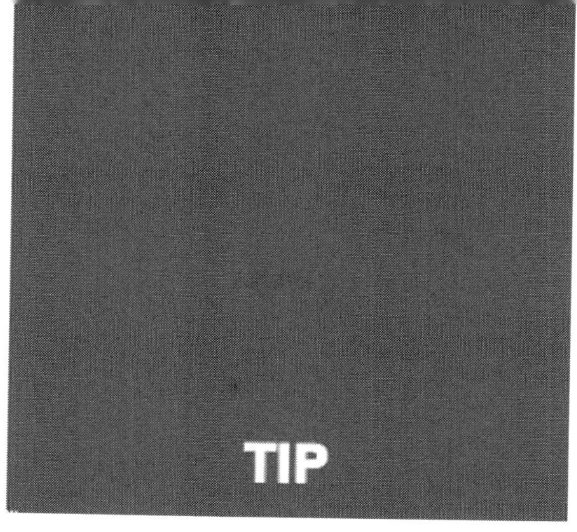

Leverage your network members within your organization by asking who have been their mentors. Get recommendations based on what they know about you and your career interests.

PLEASE SEEK TO BUILD MORE THAN ONE SPONSORING RELATIONSHIP.

We have all heard the saying "Never put all of your eggs in one basket." This could not be truer in any sponsoring relationship. Build a network of sponsors or mentors. One may take more time than the other, but relying on just one person is a bad idea. We have all seen situations where when the sponsor left the organization (or was asked to leave), so did those whom she or he publicly supported.

MAKE A LIST OF WHO YOU NEED TO KNOW AND WHY. THEN GO FIND THEM.

Who do you need to know, and how can you leverage them? What about when you're clear on what you need but don't know who you need to know to make it happen? Don't wait around to bump into someone who might fill the need. Keep your list in mind. If you don't already know John Smith, your potential mentor, but you know you need a mentor, leveraging your contacts to help you locate one (or several) is key. Often, people need to be introduced to someone, but instead of asking others to help, they wait until someone in a related field shows up and then says, "Oh, by the way, do you know...?" True success requires being proactive; this is not a proactive approach.

REPUTATION COUNTS AS YOU SEEK MENTORSHIP.
Whether your organization has a formal or informal program, if you are looking for a mentor, get to know those leaders in your organization that may qualify as good mentors. Observe and ask around. Seek those managers or leaders with a track record over time of developing people in your organization. They don't have to be in your department or function. They will stand out irrespective of where they are in your company or what they do. Always do your "mentor homework." Listen with intent and pay close attention to all information shared with you.

If your organization wants you to take a mentor who has a bad reputation in terms of ill treatment of mentees, then professionally decline the offer. That person won't treat you any better.

LOOK FOR SUCCESSFUL PEOPLE IN YOUR ORGANIZATION.

Find the successful people in your organization. If you're not sure who these people are, ask around. One easy way is to look at your organizational announcements focusing on who was promoted or who recently took on a larger role. Also, consider who was just assigned a new or important project. These assignments are often based on individuals' previous accomplishments (e.g., having a certain expertise led them to the organization supporting their work). Perhaps there was someone who advocated for them. Whatever the reason, seek them out and ask who helped them achieve their success. Is anyone helping them with their ongoing development? You will likely find a very successful person behind the person with whom you are speaking. No one achieves success alone.

Have you done any homework on the managers and leaders in your organization to know what type of mentor you would like?

HAVE YOUR LIST OF MENTORS READY.

As you talk with others, listen to their feedback and develop your list of mentors. Take note of what these individuals have to offer, their areas of expertise, etc. By developing such a list, you will have something readily available when you need a mentor. The time to look for a mentor is before you really need one. This way, when the need arises, you are prepared. Keep in mind that some on your list may change jobs, take on other roles and responsibilities or even leave your organization. You may even outgrow the need for a certain mentor's expertise. Keep your list updated.

KNOW WHAT YOU WANT IN YOUR MENTORING RELATIONSHIP. Your career goals should be clear and go beyond just the standard, "I want to get promoted" when seeking a mentoring relationship. Think about what you need a mentor to assist you with. When seeking a mentor, share what you are trying to achieve. Is it a new skill? If so, be sure it's one that will help you become better equipped and ready for the next career move you desire and deserve.

COMMUNICATE CLEARLY TO YOUR ORGANIZATION.
Talk with your manager and others responsible for your success about your goals. Tell the organization what you want. Make sure it honors your request. Be clear about what you want a mentor to help you with. Don't get stuck with one who isn't interested in your success. Always communicate clearly and often to as many people as you need to about what you want to achieve. Have one clear message. Be consistent across all conversations, lest the organization is confused about your goals and development. You want a mentor who will help you grow and achieve the right success.

If a mentoring relationship is not working out, no matter what level the mentor is, figure out a way to end the relationship gracefully and confidentially. You will get nothing out of sharing with others that you are not content.

WORK ON BUILDING THE RIGHT RELATIONSHIPS EARLY ON. Obtaining sponsorship starts with those you desire in your organization feeling comfortable about who you are and what you represent, which takes time. Find leaders who you are interested in getting to know and who you think would be interested in getting to know you. Introduce yourself. These leaders don't have to be in your particular area of the organization. Find leaders from diverse backgrounds or areas of expertise of whom the organization thinks highly.

DON'T WAIT TO BE "TAPPED ON THE SHOULDER."
It's not the sponsors' role to seek out those that they would like to provide guidance and support to within their organization. If you desire sponsorship with the benefits it affords you, then let your leadership know. More importantly, let them know why having a sponsor is essential to your overall career success. By doing this, you are signaling that you know the importance of having support to make the appropriate leadership and career moves, and you are requesting to have such support. Based on your organization's response to you, you can determine what you should do going forward with your professional career.

NOTES

NOTES

Seven

Leadership – What's It to You?

WHAT'S IT TO YOU?

This is actually a very important question. Leadership roles are excellent opportunities to demonstrate your well-rounded skills and expertise. Whether you lead a team in general or lead projects from time to time, it's in this space of leadership that you can find success.

Leadership isn't just a role or title; it's a process of engaging in goal-driven and success-oriented behaviors. Attaining a leadership role is a multifaceted endeavor. It means being much more than great at your job. Your excellence is a given in most roles, but there are many other excellent employees in your organization. Your ability to present quality leadership characteristics beforehand is how you stand out. Leadership qualities include things like the ability to prioritize (which sounds obvious, but we know in business priorities can change in a second), motivate others and transform individuals and teams. It's the ability to take the lead, be accountable and get results. Of course, leadership skills and traits must be demonstrable before the role is offered.

This chapter will offer insights, tips and words of caution to help you clarify whether you really want a leadership role and, if so, what kind of leader you want to be. This chapter will also provide you with the information you need to leverage your leadership traits and land that project lead role. In addition, we'll show you how to get noticed by important decision makers who can help you obtain the leadership role you've always wanted.

Being a leader requires a variety of skill sets and can include demonstrating basic leadership behaviors, even without the title, like conflict management, feedback (giving and receiving), accountability and solutions. It also includes many of the other skills and behaviors already laid out in the previous chapters. If you want that leadership role, you need to have the conversation, be effective in that conversation and develop the skills necessary to be recognized as the best choice for a leadership role.

Leadership roles don't often fall in your lap. Leveraging the opportunities, the mentors and sponsors, and all the other skill sets laid out in this book is what will get you noticed by important decision makers. Once you get noticed, it's up to you what you do with it. But if you follow the insights here, you'll find success.

Am I serving as a model for others to see in the organization the importance and value of serving in such a capacity?

OBSERVE HOW LEADERS IN YOUR ORGANIZATION NAVIGATE AND CONNECT WITH OTHER LEADERS.

Observing other individuals who are leaders or in leadership positions often is the best way to see and learn how they are navigating through your company. You observe and learn what helps them be successful and what hinders them. Also, it allows you to determine what leaders with whom you want to partner as you develop your network.

CULTIVATE RELATIONSHIPS ACROSS GROUPS AND FUNCTIONS OUTSIDE OF YOUR OWN.

Leaders are known to do this. It is expected. Leaders often have to do this because their given tasks often require enrolling multiple groups and various individuals. They have no choice but to mobilize commitment and create shared ownership to achieve a lofty goal. The relationships they establish and nurture outside their area or function become important and often necessary. If leaders don't do this, they may fail.

LEARN TO LEVERAGE YOUR LEADER.

Take the time to ask your leader to introduce you to people in your organization. This will give you the time to meet them and share who you are and what you do. They may not see your name on the project, but if they know what you do in your leader's group, they will more than likely know you were a part of the work in some shape or form.

If people didn't behave the way you expected or needed them to, never trusting anyone again is not the solution.

LEADERS VIEW FAILURES AS LEARNING OPPORTUNITIES AND A CHALLENGE TO DO BETTER.

It stinks to fail, but wasting time and energy feeling bad doesn't change the outcome. Every failure or misstep is an opportunity to create a new strategy. Research shows that the most successful people view failures as challenges and problems to be solved. Instead of being stuck in judgment over a negative outcome, take inventory of the event(s) in question and move on. If the issue can be revisited, create a new strategy. If not, develop an awareness of the roles everyone played and what you can do differently in future similar circumstances.

DON'T JUST TAKE A LEADERSHIP ROLE – TAKE THE RIGHT LEADERSHIP ROLE.

Everyone has an authentic style. It's important to know what yours is in the clearest possible terms. Understanding your leadership style allows you to determine where and what kind of teams you want to lead. If you're a more hands-off type of leader, for example, then leading a team of novices might not be the best place for your skills and talents. Before you decide you want to take on a leadership role, first determine your style of leadership and be clear on the kind of leader necessary for the role you seek. If it matches your style, you have a greater chance of succeeding. Once you have this experience, you will then have the opportunity to learn different styles of leadership for different projects and employees at all levels of expertise.

PRACTICE FLEXIBILITY.

Your leadership success is in part determined by consistency. However, flexibility in specific situations or with specific individuals is another piece of the success pie. Once you're clear on your general leadership style, the next step is clarifying how that style can be modified for specific interactions. If you're a project lead, which requires you to delegate, for example, you'll be interacting with a variety of personalities. While your message is clear and consistent for all members of your team, the delivery may require tweaking for different people. Leadership and the practice of leadership skills includes taking the time to assess the best way to interact with everyone and continuing to motivate them in a way that conforms to the needs of the business as well as those of the team members.

THE 4 A'S OF SUCCESSFUL LEADERSHIP

Successful leaders practice the 4 A's of leadership during a crisis:

Assess – takes a measured and objective look at what is happening
Accountability – makes no excuses; clearly knows who or what is playing a role in the current state of affairs
Accepts – acknowledges what can't be changed and focuses on strategies to make corrections
Adjusts – executes the strategies and makes adjustments along the way by using the first three A's

LEADERSHIP AND POWER ARE NOT THE SAME.

A leadership role means you have the power to control or motivate. There is no shortage of stories about leaders who get results with a demotivated and demoralized team – and high turnover is the result. Those leaders focus more on their power and less on the leadership role. Just like having a network that works for you, a truly successful leader has a team that works for her on the common goals of the organization. Regardless of the type of work you may be doing, the power to motivate others leads to greater success than using bullying tactics to get the job done.

YOU CAN DEMONSTRATE YOUR LEADERSHIP SKILLS BEFORE YOU BECOME A LEADER.

There is a term for a leader who may not have the title yet: "servant leadership," which sounds less appealing than it should. If want to get noticed as a leader, the servant leader route is one way to get there. Characteristics of servant leaders are not very different from those of any other leader; being a role model for other team members, being generous and maintaining integrity in all you do are the qualities that stand out in a servant leader. Team members look to the success you achieve by leveraging these qualities and will follow suit.

ARE YOU SURE YOU WANT A LEADERSHIP ROLE?

It's not uncommon to look upward when planning your career trajectory. Leadership means different things to different people and varies from company to company. Clarifying what a leadership role would entail in your current organization is the first step to deciding whether you want that role. Perhaps you would be better suited to a leadership role in a different organization or industry; perhaps not. Before you jump into that role, take inventory of what you want to achieve and how far you want to go. Horizontal moves are more common now than ever before. You don't have to go up to have some leadership responsibilities. Knowing how high you want to go and what exactly you want to achieve from a leadership standpoint is essential to making the career choices that best suit your desires.

Do I expect and hold not only myself but others in my organization accountable to serve as organizational bridges and connectors?

YOU SHOULDN'T DO IT ALL – EVER.

Delegating is an important part of leadership. It demonstrates desire to achieve success by identifying and utilizing the individual strengths of your team. It also provides an opportunity to hone your own leadership skills of coaching and developing. Many people, especially those new to the leadership role, may feel the need to do everything. In addition, new leaders may not yet know who the right person is for specific tasks. You need to complete projects in the best way possible, but that doesn't mean you do it all yourself. Pay attention to those around you and ask questions, but if you're trying to do it all in an effort to avoid delegating to the wrong person, you may have more problems, not less. Worse, doing everything in an effort to appear capable can lead to burnout. Delegating work is one of the most valuable skills you can master and leverage as a leader. Remember to always keep your goals as a leader in mind when you delegate.

A TRUSTED LEADER IS A SUCCESSFUL LEADER.

Trust is hard to build, but when a leader is trusted, her team is more successful. The practice of building trust begins with transparency and goodwill. Essentially, this means your team must believe that you are not only working toward success for yourself but also helping them achieve success. Being clear on what you can do, what is most likely to happen and how that affects the team as well as the bottom line will lay the foundation for gaining your team's trust. In addition, when a leader is trusted, then the team members are more likely to cooperate with one another and be more innovative. Being the leader of a team like that is what gets you noticed for greater leadership opportunities. Always check in with your team, and be open and ready for feedback.

BE INSPIRATIONAL.

Feedback is a wonderful tool, but acknowledgement can work wonders. The difference between acknowledgement and feedback is that acknowledgement doesn't come with a "but." The purpose of acknowledgement is to tell your team members (as a whole or individually) that you appreciate them. Appreciating individual efforts and recognizing a specific talent or achievement improves your team's engagement, which is an indicator of how successful your team or organization will be. Of course, everyone likes a little acknowledgement and recognition for good work – including you. Most people have had the unfortunate experience of working for leaders who didn't acknowledge them at all. You probably experienced this yourself. Now try to recall a time when you were acknowledged and how it inspired you to keep doing good work. Your team members need that as well.

STAY FOCUSED ON THE BIGGER PICTURE.

Leaders can often be overwhelmed by the desire to get everything right and prove they are the best person for the job. Insecurity is normal, but when that insecurity manifests as micromanaging, you'll have problems. You'll need to review work and coach your employees as needed, naturally. However, micromanaging is an innovation killer for your team and makes the leader's day longer and more complicated than it needs to be. Here's where you can use your listening superpower: Your team has ideas, so listen to them and discover which ones can be implemented. Ultimately, micromanagers get the job done, but they rarely advance. You want to be noticed as a leader, trusted as a leader and promoted as a leader. Remember, using leadership skills strategically and effectively will have a greater impact on your team and your career.

NOTES

NOTES

Acknowledgements

FRANCINE PARHAM

I would like to thank my collaborator extraordinaire, Dolores DeGiacomo. My son Christopher, my biggest cheerleader and light of my life. My mom, Juanita, who taught me that I can achieve anything I set my mind to. My dad, Oscar Sr., who taught me to take no prisoners. My brother Oscar Jr., who always has my back. My sisters Nikki and Lisa, two peas in a pod; Maria, who never fails to educate me, and my baby brother Mark who encouraged me to just put it all out there. Finally I want to thank my dearest friends Felicia and Christine, who have always been there for me and Aparna, your professional wisdom has been invaluable.

I want to acknowledge the network of amazing people who helped make this book possible; The Ellevate network who introduced me to my collaborator. The Black Career Women's Network for being a reference point and a role model...Go Sherry Sims. To Jessica, who taught me, if you like it, I should love it. Finally, I want to acknowledge all of the outstanding men and women I've met throughout my career who have mentored and sponsored me, who opened doors and coached me along the way. I am still a work in progress, thank you.

DOLORES DEGIACOMO:
I want to thank my collaborator, Francine Parham for helping me see beyond the horizon. I want to thank my dad for supporting me in all the many ways that only a father can and my stepmother Nancy for suffering through it. I want to thank my sisters Lisa, Valerie, and Annie for always being my best friends, my comic relief, and my sounding board. I want to thank my oldest and dearest friend Vini, who has seen me through everything!

I want to acknowledge my late hero Albert Ellis, whose technique taught me how to be challenging and compassionate at the same time. I want to acknowledge the local networks of professionals that introduced me to those amazing individuals who became friends - I'm talking about you Deirdre Ryan! Finally I want acknowledge my late brother Michael, without whom I would not have an appreciation for art and individuality.

About the Authors

Francine Parham

I am an accomplished business professional, author and the creator of Career Pocket Guides™, a series of books that provide practical insights, tools and tips for professionals to use for career success.

I speak professionally and write in various media outlets about the skills needed to be successful based on my two decades of leadership experiences, coupled with lessons learned as I navigated through several corporate environments and organizational cultures throughout the world.

The last assignment I held was a global position as vice president of human resources for Johnson & Johnson. I also worked for the General Electric Company in the capacity of vice president, beginning my career at General Mills Inc. upon completion of graduate school.

I hold master's degrees from the University of Illinois – Labor and Employment Relations and from Columbia University Graduate School of Journalism (confirmed 2017). My undergraduate degree is from Purdue University.

I am a strong advocate and supporter of the power of networks, affiliate groups, sponsorship and the development of strategic network connections. I believe that your professional networks and the connections you make throughout your career serve as the foundation of your success. No one achieves anything alone.

I am honored to be the mother of an entrepreneur and owner of two online marketplace communities, ContractRight.com and LogonTutor.com. My son, Christopher Parham-Darabi, is a graduate of the University of Cincinnati.

About the Authors

Dolores DeGiacomo

I am a leadership development coach, consultant and speaker focusing on developing mastery over success-oriented thinking and behavior patterns. I created the Power Up! coaching method to enable professionals to get clear on their goals and develop executable strategies for achievement. My clients are professionals of all levels, from emerging leaders to executives to entrepreneurs.

I can be found writing and speaking on topics related to leadership and goal-focused thinking and behavior patterns. You can find my articles on Forbes.com and HuffingtonPost.com as well as LinkedIn.

I have more than a decade of experience in corporate staff management as well as managing union-represented employees at Verizon Telecom. I founded my consulting practice in 2009 and began teaching undergraduate psychology at Kean University that same year. In addition to my experience and knowledge of what it's like to be a frontline manager in a male-dominated industry, I stay focused on what's happening in the lives of millennials through mentoring as well as teaching. A quality education, I believe, is only part the equation for success. In that vein, I work with my students and young clients to ensure that they are well prepared for their future and their careers.

I hold a master's degree from Pace University in NYC in psychology as well as a master's degree in clinical social work from Rutgers University.

33163289R00102

Made in the USA
Middletown, DE
02 July 2016